The *Supernatural* Language

Why You Should Speak in Tongues

ROBERTS LIARDON

Unless otherwise indicated, all Scripture quotations are taken from the *King James Version* of the Holy Bible.

Scripture quotations marked (NKJV) are taken from the *New King James Version* © 1979, 1980, 1982, 1984 by Thomas Nelson, Inc. Used by permission. All rights reserved.

THE SUPERNATURAL LANGUAGE
Why You Should Speak in Tongues
Roberts Liardon Ministries
P. O. Box 4215
Sarasota, FL 34230

E-mail: info@robertsliardon.org
www.RobertsLiardon.org

ISBN: 978-1-7336062-3-3
eBook ISBN: 978-1-7336062-4-0

Copyright © 1999, 2022 by Roberts Liardon

Editorial Consultant: Cynthia D. Hansen
Text Design: Lisa Simpson, www.SimpsonProductions.net

Printed in the United States of America. All rights reserved. No part of this book may be reproduced or transmitted in any form or by any means, electronic, or mechanical — including photocopying, recording, or by any information storage and retrieval system — without permission in writing from the Publisher. Please direct your inquiries to info@robertsliardon.org.

CONTENTS

1 Welcome to the Wonderful World of Tongues 5
2 What Jesus Said About the Holy Spirit 13
3 What Happened When the Holy Spirit Came 23
4 The Holy Spirit and Tongues in the Book of Acts 29
5 The Apostle Paul's Experience With the Holy Spirit
    and Tongues 35
6 The Benefits of Praying in Tongues 41
7 Your Prayer Language Should Grow 51
8 Tongues Help Our Infirmities 57
9 The Gift of Tongues and the Gift
    of Interpretation of Tongues 73
10 Interpreting Your Personal Prayer Language 81
11 Diversities of Tongues 87
12 Common Sense With the Use of Tongues 99
13 How To Minister the Baptism in the Holy Spirit 105
14 How To Receive the Holy Spirit and Speak
    With Tongues 109

About the Author 113

Chapter 1

Welcome to the Wonderful World of Tongues

While preaching in New York many years ago, I had one of the most unique experiences of my life. I received a phone call from a few pastors in Long Island who wanted me to come and share my testimony of going to Heaven at an evangelistic crusade they were holding.

"Brother Roberts," the pastors said, "we believe you're supposed to be the one to give the message and throw the net of salvation."

"I'd love to do it," I replied.

When I flew in, the pastors picked me up and drove me to the hotel where they were holding the meeting. The meeting was on neutral turf, in a hotel ballroom that seated approximately 500 people. I had arrived a little late, so I quickly changed my clothes and went downstairs to join the meeting that was already in progress. Every seat was taken. There were even people in the back of the room standing. The ballroom was packed.

When I stepped behind the pulpit, I began by telling the people how the Lord had showed me a part of Heaven when I was a little boy. I told them what I saw and how I felt, as I normally do when I share my Heaven testimony.

As I was speaking, I noticed a woman sitting about five rows back. Beside her were three young men dressed in black leather and chains. The way these teenagers dressed didn't bother me, but they stood out because they were the only people in the building dressed that way.

Usually it takes me 45 minutes to tell my Heaven story and 20 minutes to give the altar call. But 30 minutes into my message, the Lord interrupted me. *"Call out those three young men and have them stand in front of you,"* He said.

I had enough sense to obey God, but I was really apprehensive about it. "You three, come up here please," I said, pointing my finger as confidently as I could in their direction.

To my surprise, the three tough-looking teenagers got up, walked straight down the aisle, and stood in front of the pulpit. I didn't know what God wanted me to do next, so I just stood there awhile as they looked at me, and I looked back at them.

The seconds seemed like long minutes as the four of us just stood there looking at each other. Meanwhile, I was trying to act spiritual — because that's what a minister does when he doesn't know what else to do. But truth be told, I was getting

Welcome to the Wonderful World of Tongues

really uncomfortable. I knew enough about obeying the Holy Spirit to do only what He told me to do, but at that moment, it seemed like He had left me hanging.

There I was, standing in front of 500 New Yorkers trying to look spiritual, when the woman I had noticed earlier suddenly fell out of her chair, face forward, into the middle of the aisle. She hit the ground with a loud thud and scared the whole crowd! There were no "cloth workers" in that meeting, and when this woman fell, she landed with her dress hiked up a little bit — not very high, but enough to make me nervous!

By this time, we were so far into this strange event that there was no way out. I couldn't sermonize about the situation, and I couldn't praise my way out — I just had to flow with it. I knew it was God, but I didn't want to look at the pastors, because I was sure my days of Long Island ministry had come to an abrupt conclusion. They had wanted an evangelistic meeting. They *hadn't* asked for a woman to bolt out of her chair and fall face down in the middle of the aisle with her nose buried in the carpet!

The woman didn't even move; she just lay there. The three young men in leather looked down at the woman lying on the ground and then back at me. Meanwhile, I just looked at all of them, trying to stay calm and to keep looking spiritual.

On the outside, I was smiling, but on the inside, I was talking *seriously* to the Lord: *Help me, God! Show up, show up, show up! Please help me out of this mess!* (It seems funny now, but it wasn't funny then!)

Then came another surprise! The woman whose nose was buried in the carpet began to pray loudly in the most unusual tongue I'd ever heard in my life. It sounded like a mixture of Chinese and some kind of strange African dialect. She prayed in that unusual-sounding tongue for about ten minutes without stopping.

The Bible says to watch and pray (Matt. 26:41) — so I watched, and the woman prayed! And the whole crowd watched as well! No one went to the bathroom or left to go home early, and not one baby in the room cried. No one moved.

Suddenly one of the three teenagers in front of me fell flat on the floor. It startled me so much, I jumped. All my attention had been on the woman lying on her face in the aisle. I had forgotten all about the three teenagers in leather! When the young man fell over, he rolled up in a little ball and began to cry with deep, gut-wrenching sobs.

So at that point, we had two shows going on in the room — a woman on her face in the aisle, praying in loud and unusual-sounding tongues, and a teenager dressed in leather, rolled up in a little ball crying!

This went on for 15 minutes or so, and I just stood and watched. Whenever the woman stopped praying as hard, the young man stopped crying and tried to catch his breath. When she'd resumed praying hard again, his loud weeping would start up again too. The two would go at it in three- or four-minute rounds. Whenever the woman prayed in tongues fervently, the teenager cried like somebody was beating him up.

I was raised as a Pentecostal, and I had seen some unusual things. But I had never seen anything like this before!

About 45 minutes into this dramatic episode, the woman suddenly stopped praying, pulled herself up to her knees, and raised her hands halfway to the Lord. As she knelt there with her eyes closed, her makeup all messed up, and one clip-on earring hanging out of place, this woman began singing in tongues and interpreting her tongues back to herself. Then without warning, she calmly got up like everything was normal, returned to her seat, closed her eyes, and sat there with clasped hands in her lap.

My attention had been riveted on the woman during all of this. When I looked over to see what was happening with the three teenagers dressed in leather, the two young men still standing had moved over to the side to distance themselves from what was happening. As for the young man on the floor, when he was finally able to catch his breath, he lifted his head and tried to focus his eyes. After he had regained enough strength to get up, he walked over to the edge of the platform where I was standing. All sweaty and red-faced, he tilted his head to look up at me and said, "Sir, I think I need to get saved."

Suddenly the crowd went wild in rejoicing! They acted like someone had just scored a touchdown at a football game! This young man was saved and filled with the Holy Spirit that night. It was almost as though God had orchestrated that entire meeting just for him!

God Knows What Kind of Prayer Is Needed

Why did I tell this story? To show you how God gives diversities of tongues to bring victory in every situation we face! In this woman's case, the Holy Spirit knew what kind of intercession, what level of intensity, and what type of divine expression was needed to get this young man delivered.

I found out after the meeting that the teenager was the woman's son. His father had hurt him deeply when he divorced his mother. In the aftermath of the divorce, this young man began to get rebellious and at times refused to come home on the weekends.

The mother had tried everything to help her son, including counseling, but he only got worse. Thank God, she knew about the diversities of tongues! That night the Holy Spirit helped her pray in a way that brought a great victory to her family.

In this woman's case, the Holy Spirit knew what kind of intercession, what level of intensity, and what type of divine expression was needed to get this young man delivered.

Exploring the Realms of Speaking in Other Tongues

The world of tongues in all their diversities is one of the great spiritual frontiers that God's children will continue to press into until Jesus returns. There is more to the realm of praying in tongues than anyone has yet discovered. If the Lord tarries and we all live out our lives on the earth, we still will not have exhausted the subject of speaking in unknown tongues when it's time for us to move to Heaven.

The purpose of this book is to help you gain accurate revelation concerning the role of tongues and of their diversities of expression in your life as you seek to fulfill God's plan and purposes. I wrote this book to help you understand that the baptism in the Holy Spirit, with the evidence of speaking in tongues, should be a normal part of your Christian life. In fact, speaking in tongues helps you be more normal than you've ever been before!

The world of tongues in all their diversities is one of the great spiritual frontiers that God's children will continue to press into until Jesus returns.

The devil doesn't want you to pray in tongues. He wants to keep you ignorant of tongues and their diversities so the Holy Spirit's power won't be able to flow through you in the fullness that God intends.

But the truth is, every person born into this world needs to be born again and then immediately receive the baptism in the Holy Spirit with the evidence of speaking in other tongues. As we will see, nothing is more beautiful than having a heavenly language flow out of an earthen vessel to do a supernatural work.

We will begin our scriptural journey into the wonderful world of tongues by exploring what Jesus said about the Holy Spirit.

Nothing is more beautiful than having a heavenly language flow out of an earthen vessel to do a supernatural work.

Chapter 2

What Jesus Said About the Holy Spirit

> If ye love me, keep my commandments. And I will pray the Father, and *he shall give you another Comforter*, that he may abide with you for ever; even the Spirit of truth; whom the world cannot receive, because it seeth him not, neither knoweth him: but ye know him; for he dwelleth with you, and shall be in you.
>
> John 14:15-17

Here Jesus described the Holy Spirit as the Comforter. In this passage of Scripture, Jesus was preparing His disciples for a great transition: He was about to leave the earth, and the Holy Spirit was about to be poured out.

Notice here that Jesus said the Father would give the disciples "another Comforter" (John 14:16). Who was the first

Comforter? Jesus! The disciples looked to Jesus as their Helper, Guide, and Teacher. Jesus loved them, instructed them, confronted them, strengthened them, and revealed truths to them.

And what Jesus was to the disciples, the Holy Spirit is to you and me today.

Not a 'Fair-Weather Friend'

Jesus promised the Comforter would "…abide with you for ever" (John 14:16). In other words, the Holy Spirit isn't going to fly away on a whim when you least expect it. He is like super glue; He sticks to you! He'll *never* leave you or forsake you (*see* John 14:18; Heb. 13:5)!

Of course, if you consistently resist the Holy Spirit and run to do evil, He will eventually let you do it. But even then, He will always be there to help you if you cry out to Him.

It's good to know that the Holy Spirit abides with you forever. That means He will be with you through thick and thin, through good times *and* bad times. The Holy Spirit is not a fair-weather friend! It doesn't matter whether the sun is out and everything is fine or you are facing the greatest challenge of your life, He will never act like a distant relative.

The Spirit and the World Don't Date!

Look at what Jesus said about the Comforter's role: "…He shall give you another Comforter, that he may abide with you for ever, even *the Spirit of truth*; whom the world cannot receive…" (John 14:16-17).

Religious devils and worldly people sometimes lie and try to deceive you, but the Holy Spirit *cannot* lie. He is the Spirit of truth.

Jesus also let us know that the Holy Spirit is the Spirit of truth *"...whom the world cannot receive...."* In other words, the Holy Spirit and the spirit of the world don't date! They don't plan a midnight rendezvous. In fact, they don't get along at all!

If you're filled with the Holy Spirit, you won't love the things of this present world (*see* 1 John 2:15). You won't have a mixture of the world and the Holy Spirit in you.

"Well, I love the Lord, but I do what I want during the week."

People who have that attitude are both fools and religious backsliders. Some people will go to hell with their prayer beads in their hands, saying, "But I prayed!" They may have recited their memorized prayers, but if they never lived the Christian life and got right with God, they just played religious games.

"But I go to church!"

So does the devil! In fact, he even sings in the choir! You can't use your Sunday attendance at church as an excuse to ease your conscience for how you live the rest of the week.

"Yes, but my grandmother is a praying person."

Well, *she'll* probably go to Heaven, but you won't unless you get right with God for yourself.

"Well, she'll pray me into Heaven."

That's not the way it works. No one can pray you into Heaven! People can pray you into the consciousness of what it will take to get to Heaven, and they may be able to hold back a lot of self-inflicted troubles in your life. But no one can "piggyback" you into Heaven. You have to fall at the foot of the Cross, cry out to God, and be cleansed with the blood of Jesus Christ. You have to get right with Him, and you have to do it for yourself.

> No one can "piggyback" you into Heaven.
> You have to fall at the foot of the Cross, cry out to God,
> and be cleansed with the blood of Jesus Christ.
> You have to get right with Him,
> and you have to do it for yourself.

JOHNNY CARSON MEETS KATHRYN KUHLMAN

We saw that Jesus called the Holy Spirit the Spirit of truth "...whom the world cannot receive" (John 14:17). The world cannot receive the Spirit of truth unless they call upon the Lord Jesus and receive Him as Savior. They cannot receive the Holy Spirit because those in the world "...seeth Him not...." Sinners live by sense knowledge, but Christians live by faith in the Bible and by the inward witness of the Holy Spirit.

This point was made years ago on national television when Johnny Carson, the famous late-night talk-show host, invited Kathryn Kuhlman to be a guest on the show. During Kathyrn's segment, Johnny asked her how she knew when the Holy Spirit was in the room.

"You can feel Him," she answered.

"Yes, but you can't see Him," Johnny replied.

Kathryn responded, "You can't see the wind either, but you know when the wind is blowing. You can feel the wind, and you can watch it blow things around.

"It's the same with the Holy Spirit. When the Spirit of God is in the room, you'll start seeing manifestations of His presence. People will cry and humble themselves before the Lord. They'll get healed; devils will come out; and the gifts of the Spirit will begin manifesting."

HE WILL GUIDE YOU INTO ALL VICTORY

In John 16, we read something else that Jesus said about the Holy Spirit:

> **"I still have many things to say to you, but you cannot bear them now. However, when He, the Spirit of truth, has come, He will guide you into all truth; for He will not speak on His own authority, but whatever He hears He will speak; and He will tell you things to come."**
>
> **John 16:12-13 NKJV**

Notice what Jesus said in verse 12: "I still have many things to say to you, but you cannot bear them now." The Holy Spirit has a great deal that He would like to reveal to God's people, but He can't because they aren't preparing themselves for it.

You have to position yourself correctly in the natural and in the Spirit if you want to partake of the deeper things of God (*see* 1 Corinthians 2:10).

Look at John 16:13 (NKJV) again: "However, when He, the Spirit of truth, has come, He will guide you into *all truth*; for He will not speak on His own authority, but whatever He hears He will speak; and He will tell you things to come." *All truth* is another way of saying *all victory.*

The Holy Spirit will never guide you into defeat! He will always guide you into victory, success, accomplishment, abundant life, soundness, happiness, and security — both in the Spirit and in the natural.

The Holy Spirit will tell you what decisions to make in business so you won't go broke every other month. He'll tell you those whom you're *not* to do business with so you can have peace of mind when you go home to kiss your wife and hug the kids. He'll tell you whether the $20,000 investment you are considering would profit you or whether you'd lose it all. He'll tell you what house to buy, when to buy it, and how much to pay.

When the Holy Spirit is helping you, you'll get a good deal, no matter what the real-estate agents have to say about it!

The Holy Spirit will never guide you into defeat! He will always guide you into victory, success, accomplishment, abundant life, soundness, happiness, and security — both in the Spirit and in the natural.

The Holy Spirit will show you what to do in every circumstance of life. He will even show you where to have a nice vacation! Sometimes He will say, *"No, don't go there this year; go here instead."*

That happened to me. I was going to visit some friends and take a little vacation, and the Holy Spirit said, *"No, don't go there at this time; it's not right. Go someplace else."* He didn't tell me where to go; He just told me to go somewhere else.

And I had a great vacation somewhere else that year! I really enjoyed it. If I had disobeyed the Holy Spirit, I probably would have found myself in the middle of some difficulty. I didn't ask Him why He wanted me to change my plans, because I really didn't need to know. I just obeyed Him and had a good time.

The Holy Spirit doesn't always reveal the intimate details of a situation — because in some cases, *it's none of your business.* He tells you only what He wants you to know and nothing else. You just have to learn to relax and trust Him. If He says, *"No, don't do that right now,"* just obey Him and be happy about it.

Trust Him to never lead you into failure, defeat, error, or deception. He's there to protect your life, not destroy it.

Jesus said, "...He will *guide* you..." (John 16:13), which means the Holy Spirit will not pick you up and sovereignly place you in the will of God; He will only help you get there. He will show you which roads to take and which roads to avoid.

If you listen to the Spirit of God, He will get you to where you belong. He'll never lead you astray.

The Holy Spirit will not pick you up and sovereignly place you in the will of God; He will only help you get there. He will show you which roads to take and which roads to avoid.

HE WILL SHOW YOU THINGS TO COME

Jesus went on to say that the Holy Spirit "...will not speak on His own authority; but whatever He hears He will speak..." (John 16:13 NKJV). In other words, the Holy Spirit doesn't have an ego problem. He doesn't tell everyone, *"I was there when the world was made. I'm just as important as the Father! I deserve some of the credit because I'm the Holy Spirit!"*

The Holy Spirit doesn't act like humans. He doesn't have a pride problem at all. He has come for two main purposes: to reveal Jesus in the earth and to empower believers.

In verse 14 (NKJV), Jesus went on to say of the Holy Spirit, "He will glorify Me...." In other words, the Holy Spirit will lift up Jesus. He will reveal Jesus to you and show you how to make Jesus your personal Friend. The Holy Spirit has also come to empower you — to be your Guide, your Comforter, and your Helper in life — and it's up to you to let Him do it.

To whom is the Holy Spirit listening? He's listening to the Father, and He's listening to the Son. Whatever the Spirit of God hears them saying, He will reveal to you — if you stay close to Him and learn to discern His voice in your spirit. He will sometimes let you in on the plans of the Father and the Son.

The Holy Spirit give you glimpses into what is being sent from Heaven to the earth. He has access to all communication between the Father and the Son. He has the ability to observe and know what's being planned, because He's a part of it.

The Holy Spirit give you glimpses into what is being sent from Heaven to the earth. He has the ability to observe and know what's being planned, because He's a part of it.

Jesus said that the Holy Spirit would show us things to come (John 16:13). That means the Holy Spirit will show you things to come on different levels of life. He will show you things to come in your family. He will show you things to come in your church. He will show you things to come in your community, in the nation, in the world, and in the realm of the spirit.

The Holy Spirit will roll back the curtains of the future and show you what's about to take place. He likes doing that, because that's what Jesus sent Him to do.

Chapter 3

What Happened When the Holy Spirit Came

> And when the day of Pentecost was fully come, they were all with one accord in one place. And suddenly there came a sound from heaven as of a rushing mighty wind, and it filled all the house where they were sitting. And there appeared unto them cloven tongues like as of fire and it sat upon each of them. And they were all filled with the Holy Spirit, and began to speak with other tongues, as the Spirit gave them utterance.
>
> Acts 2:1-4

A group of 120 disciples of Jesus had been praying and waiting before the Lord in that upper room ever since He ascended into Heaven ten days earlier. We know the identity of some of those present that day. Of course, the 12 apostles were there, including Matthias, who took the place of

Judas Iscariot (*see* Acts 1:26). Barsabas, the other disciple who was considered in replacing Judas Iscariot, was also present (*see* Acts 1:23-25). The 120 also included Jesus' mother Mary and His brothers, as well as other women who had followed Jesus during His earthly ministry (*see* Acts 1:14-15).

Acts 2:1 says that all those present in that upper room on the Day of Pentecost were "...with one accord in one place." That's a miracle in itself! To get that many Christians in one accord usually takes a sovereign act of God!

Here we see that God wants His people to come into the unity of the Spirit. However, true unity is not just outward conformity; it is established in our hearts through the inner workings of the Holy Spirit.

No Tarrying Needed

Prior to Jesus' ascension, He commanded the disciples to "tarry" in Jerusalem for the promise of the Holy Spirit (*see* Luke 24:49). Many Christians through the years have gotten hung up on that word "tarrying." Some have tarried so long that they died without receiving the promise of the Spirit!

The disciples tarried in that upper room because they were waiting for the promise of the Holy Spirit. Now that we are on the other side of Pentecost, we don't need to tarry to be baptized in the Holy Spirit. We can receive the infilling of the Spirit and begin speaking in tongues the very moment we ask for that precious Gift — because the Spirit of God has already come!

"And suddenly there came a sound from heaven as of a rushing mighty wind..." (Acts 2:2). That word "rushing" indicates that the Holy Spirit was in a hurry to get here. He didn't fly around Jupiter, visit Mars, and then circle the sun for a little vacation! He came straight from Heaven at an accelerated pace. He couldn't wait to get here to *baptize, fill, empower, teach, guide,* and *help* believers in Christ! This shows us the Holy Spirit's earnest desire to provide God's people with His divine assistance.

The word "mighty" also shows us that the Holy Spirit didn't come floating into the upper room like "Casper the friendly ghost." He came with *great strength and power*! He came as a "…rushing mighty wind, and it filled all the house where they were sitting" (Acts 2:2). This shows us that *strength* is one of the predominant characteristics of the Holy Spirit's personality.

It's important to note here that when Jesus was baptized in the Holy Spirit in Matthew 3, the Holy Spirit came upon Him gently in the form of a dove (*see* Matt. 3:16). But on the Day of Pentecost, the Holy Spirit came in the form of a "rushing mighty wind" (Acts 2:2).

This reveals the dual nature of the Holy Spirit. He has both a gentle side and a mighty side. We have to be willing for *both* qualities of the Holy Spirit to manifest through us at different times according to His leading.

They All Spoke in Tongues

In Acts 2:3 (NKJV), we read: "Then there appeared to them *divided tongues, as of fire,* and one sat upon each of them." The holy fire of God's anointing sparks a supernatural zeal, and it also has a purifying effect. It will burn up the "chaff" in your life and give you strength to live a holy life before God.

What did the 120 do when they were filled with the Holy Spirit? They began to speak in tongues — *all* of them.

The holy fire of God's anointing sparks a supernatural zeal, and it also has a purifying effect. It will burn up the "chaff" in your life and give you strength to live a holy life before God.

And they were *all* filled with the Holy Spirit and began to speak with other tongues, *as the Spirit gave them utterance.*

Acts 2:4

"Now, Brother Roberts, you don't want to go too far."

Yes, I do! I want to go all the way with God! I want to get everyone I meet baptized in the Holy Spirit with the evidence of speaking in other tongues!

The Scriptures are clear: When you are baptized in or filled to overflowing with the Spirit of God, you will speak in other tongues (*see* Acts 2:4; 10:45-56; 19:6). If you don't speak in other tongues, you're not full of the Holy Spirit. It's that simple. You may be *indwelt* by the Spirit and have an inner witness that you are a child of God. If that is the case, the Holy Spirit will work with you as much as He is able according to the level you allow Him to work. But that doesn't mean you're *filled with* and *empowered by* the Holy Spirit, even though that experience is available to you as a believer.

Acts 2:4 says, "And they were all filled with the Holy Spirit *and*...." The word "and" is a conjunction, which means that whatever follows goes with whatever preceded it. So we know that the next part of the sentence, which says, "...*and* began to speak with other tongues..." is directly connected to the first part — the infilling of the Holy Spirit.

The Scriptures are clear: When you are baptized in or filled to overflowing with the Spirit of God, you will speak in other tongues.

"Brother Roberts, are you saying I'm a second-rate Christian if I haven't been baptized in the Holy Spirit and don't speak with other tongues?"

No! But I *am* saying that the Holy Spirit is not working in your life to full capacity.

"Well, you're making me feel like a second-rate Christian."

No, I'm trying to help you receive all God has freely provided. The baptism in the Holy Spirit, with the evidence of speaking in tongues, is rightfully yours as a child of God.

I believe there are some Christians who asked for and received the baptism in the Holy Spirit but have not yet released the supernatural language of the Holy Spirit they received with that gift by speaking in other tongues. This is mainly because of an absence of knowledge. But I believe the full baptism of the Holy Spirit is always evidenced by speaking in tongues. You'll see this is true as we examine different portions of Scripture in the next chapter.

Chapter 4

The Holy Spirit and Tongues in the Book of Acts

Let's look at some other examples in the book of Acts of the baptism in the Holy Spirit with the evidence of tongues. In Acts 10, we read the account of what happened when the Lord directed Peter to go preach Christ to the household of the Roman centurion Cornelius:

> While Peter was still speaking these words, the Holy Spirit fell upon all those who heard the word. And those of the circumcision who believed were astonished, as many as came with Peter, because the gift of the Holy Spirit had been poured out on the Gentiles also. For they heard them speak with tongues and magnify God.
>
> Acts 10:44-46 NKJV

The hearing of the Word causes the Holy Spirit to move. Throughout the New Testament, whenever people heard the Word, they were saved, healed, and delivered.

Here in these verses, when the Gentiles heard the Word preached to them, they received the *gift* of the Holy Spirit. The term "gift" tells us that the infilling of the Holy Spirit is free. We can't buy Him. We can't act holy enough or do enough good works to *earn* Him. All we can do is receive Him.

We see in this verse two key truths: 1) Speaking in tongues helps our magnification of God; and 2) the baptism in the Holy Spirit and speaking in tongues are received together in the same experience.

The infilling of the Holy Spirit is free. We can't buy Him. We can't act holy enough or do enough good works to earn Him. All we can do is receive Him.

What happened when these Gentiles received the baptism in the Holy Spirit? We find the answer in Acts 10:46 (NKJV): "For they *heard* them speak with tongues and magnify God." That phrase "for they heard them" is the opposite of *not* hearing. In other words, the members of Cornelius' household were speaking loudly enough for those who were with Peter to hear and be astonished that Gentiles now were speaking in tongues.

Some people today have a similar way of thinking. They say, "Well, only special people can speak in tongues. It's not for us." But this passage of Scripture tells us that, after receiving salvation, *anyone* can receive the infilling of the Holy Spirit and speak with other tongues. And if you're truly filled with the Holy Spirit, you will speak in other tongues loudly enough for those around you to hear!

Once you're born again, you'll have the witness of the Spirit within you, and the Spirit will help you according to the level you allow Him to help you. So if you want to be empowered to the full capacity that the Lord desires, you need to receive the infilling of the Holy Spirit and pray in other tongues boldly and unashamedly.

And if you're truly filled with the Holy Spirit, you will speak in other tongues loudly enough for those around you to hear!

Another Witness

The Bible says, "...In the mouth of two or three witnesses shall every word be established" (2 Cor. 13:1). So let's look at another instance in Acts where people were baptized in the Holy Spirit:

> **And it happened, while Apollos was at Corinth, that Paul, having passed through the upper regions, came to Ephesus. And finding some disciples he said to them, "Did you receive the Holy Spirit when you believed?" So they said to him, "We have not so much as heard whether there is a Holy Spirit." And he said to them, "Into what then were you baptized?" So they said, "Into John's baptism."**

> **Then Paul said, "John indeed baptized with a baptism of repentance, saying to the people that they should believe on Him who would come after him, that is, on Christ Jesus." When they heard this, they were baptized in the name of the Lord Jesus. And when Paul had laid hands on them, the Holy Spirit came upon them, and they spoke with tongues and prophesied.**
>
> **Acts 19:1-6 NKJV**

Sometimes when I read in the book of Acts about the way the apostle Paul lived and ministered, I think, *Lord, that sounds so exciting!* This account in Acts 19 is one of those instances. Verse 1 says that Paul "found" this group of disciples, which means that before they came across Paul's path, he didn't know they were there.

Because these men had believed in John's preaching about repentance, they easily received what Paul had to say about the Holy Spirit. Notice that Paul thought it was important to make sure these disciples were filled with the Holy Spirit. It wasn't an afterthought; it was the first thing he asked them: "...Did you receive the Holy Spirit when you believed?" (Acts 19:2 NKJV).

"We don't know about any Holy Spirit."

Paul thought it was important to make sure these disciples were filled with the Holy Spirit. It wasn't an afterthought; it was the first thing he asked them.

Their answer probably caught Paul off-guard. "What baptism are you baptized under?" Paul asked.

"John's baptism."

These disciples hadn't been present for the outpouring of the Holy Spirit that happened in the upper room on the Day of Pentecost. They hadn't heard Peter or the other 120 preach about Jesus. So Paul explained to them, "John truly baptized with the baptism of repentance, but do you remember what John said? He said that you are to believe on the One who comes after him, and that One is Jesus Christ" (*see* Acts 19:4).

What did the disciples do after Paul told them about Jesus? They believed! And what happened when he told them about receiving the Holy Spirit? They were filled with the Spirit, and they spoke with tongues and prophesied!

So Acts 19:6 (NKJV) is our third witness: "...The Holy Spirit came upon them, and they spoke with tongues and prophesied."

But that's not all — I have another witness for you. In the next chapter, we will see that even the great apostle Paul spoke in tongues when he received the Holy Spirit.

CHAPTER 5

The Apostle Paul's Experience With the Holy Spirit and Tongues

In Acts 9, we find the story of the apostle Paul's conversion, when he was still called Saul of Tarsus. Saul was traveling by horse to Damascus with a company of men, when — *bam!* — suddenly he was knocked off his horse, given a vision of Jesus, and blinded by a heavenly light. *Now, that's a supernatural event!*

It gets even more dramatic when you consider Saul's occupation before this occurrence.

Saul was persecuting Christians, traveling to Damascus with the intent of putting them in jail and even killing them.

Then God sent His lightnings from His throne room and interrupted Saul's evil agenda!

> "Now it happened, as I journeyed and came near Damascus at about noon, suddenly a great light from heaven shone around me. And I fell to the ground and heard a voice saying to me, 'Saul, Saul, why are you persecuting Me?' So I answered, 'Who are You, Lord?' And He said to me, 'I am Jesus of Nazareth, whom you are persecuting.' And those who were with me indeed saw the light and were afraid, but they did not hear the voice of Him who spoke to me."
>
> Acts 22:6-9 NKJV

Saul was persecuting Christians, traveling to Damascus with the intent of putting them in jail and even killing them. Then God sent His lightnings from His throne room and interrupted Saul's evil agenda!

Everyone who was with Saul saw the heavenly light, but Saul was the only one who *heard and saw Jesus.*

> Then Saul arose from the ground, and when his eyes were opened he saw no one. But they led him by the hand and brought him into Damascus. And he was three days without sight, and neither ate nor drank.
>
> Acts 9:8-9 NKJV

Saul was probably in a state of shock after what he had experienced. For three days and three nights, he did nothing but fast and pray.

I'd fast and pray, too, if I was knocked off my horse, had a divine encounter with Jesus, and was struck blind! I'd pray loud enough for the whole world to hear!

That's what Saul did at the beginning of his experience with Jesus. And God answered his prayers through a man named Ananias:

> **Now there was a certain disciple at Damascus named Ananias; and to him the Lord said in a vision, "Ananias." And he said, "Here I am, Lord."**
>
> **Acts 9:10 NKJV**

I'm so thankful for people of maturity in the Spirit who can respond properly during a heavenly visitation. In the Scriptures, every time angels showed up, they said, "Fear not!" because most people in that situation are overwhelmed by fear.

If an angel ever appears to you, don't let yourself get all flustered, thinking, *Oh my God, there's an angel in front of me! What am I supposed to do?* Just calm yourself down and listen to what the angel has to say.

You can tell Ananias was mature by the way he responded during the visitation. He simply said, "Here I am, Lord!" In other words, he was saying, "I'm available! What is it You want me to do?"

> **So the Lord said to him, "Arise and go to the street called Straight, and inquire at the house of Judas for one called Saul of Tarsus, for behold, he is praying. And in a vision he has seen a man named Ananias coming in and putting his hand on him, so that he might receive his sight."**
>
> **Acts 9:11-12 NKJV**

So Saul of Tarsus had two key visitors in his salvation experience: 1) the One who knocked him off his high horse on the road to Damascus, and 2) the one who brought comfort to him a few days later, showing him that God was going to take care of his blindness.

> **Then Ananias answered, "Lord, I have heard from many about this man, how much harm he has done to Your saints in Jerusalem. And here he has authority from the chief priests to bind all who call on Your name."**
>
> **But the Lord said to him, "Go, for he is a chosen vessel of Mine to bear My name before Gentiles, kings, and the children of Israel. For I will show him how many things he must suffer for My name's sake."**
>
> **And Ananias went his way and entered the house, and laying his hands on him he said, "Brother Saul, the Lord Jesus, who appeared to you on the road as you came has sent me that you may receive your sight and be filled with the Holy Spirit."**
>
> **Acts 9:13-17 NKJV**

Here we see that Saul was filled the Holy Spirit when this great servant of God laid his hands on him. And I believe that at that very moment, Saul began to speak in other tongues — because there's no reason why his infilling of the Holy Spirit would be different than all the others in the book of Acts.

Some use this particular verse as an excuse not to speak in tongues when they receive the baptism in the Holy Spirit, because it doesn't actually say here that Saul spoke in tongues. But later as the apostle Paul, he wrote more about tongues than anyone else in the Bible. In fact, in First Corinthians 14:18 (NKJV), Paul wrote, "I thank my God I speak with tongues more than you all." It is obvious by Paul's statement that he didn't speak in tongues just one time. He prayed in tongues *a lot*.

So when we consider Acts 9:17 and First Corinthians 14:18 together, we can conclude that Paul (then Saul) spoke with tongues when Ananias laid his hands on him. And he didn't speak in tongues just one time either. When Paul wrote, "I thank my God I speak with tongues more than you all," he implied that it was a continual occurrence in his life. Speaking in tongues was normal to Paul — and he flowed in it daily. And if the apostle Paul spoke with tongues as a normal part of his daily life, we should too!

It's important to note that Paul wrote this first epistle to the Corinthian believers to bring them into order because of wrong practices and the misuse of certain operations of the gifts of the Spirit in the church. Paul offered the Corinthian congregation his instructions in these chapters to help them use tongues more effectively.

**Speaking in tongues was normal to Paul —
and he flowed in it daily. And if the apostle Paul spoke
with tongues as a normal part of his daily life,
we should too!**

Some people have tried to use certain verses in First Corinthians 14 to discourage people from speaking in tongues. But Paul was not reprimanding the Corinthians for speaking in tongues; he was giving them instruction so that tongues could be more beneficial in their lives.

A HOLY COMPETITION

I have a holy competition going between me and the apostle Paul, and I won't know if I've won it until I get to Heaven. I want it to be said of me that Roberts Liardon prayed in tongues more than all — including the apostle Paul! I think that's a holy and good competition, and I want to enlist you to join in! Let's all try to outdo Paul.

"How will we know when we've done it?"

We won't know until we get to Heaven, so we'll just have to keep praying in tongues. When we all get there, we'll see who won — and regardless who it is, we'll all rejoice in how much was accomplished on earth by this holy competition to see who could pray in tongues *more than all*!

Chapter 6

The Benefits of Praying in Tongues

If you've listened at all to what I've preached over the years, you know I'm a strong advocate of the development of people's prayer lives — especially in this area of praying in tongues. I often emphasize tongues and strong prayer during my messages because I know how beneficial these practices are in the life of a believer.

Here are just a few of the benefits of praying in tongues.

1. Tongues Are the Evidence of Infilling

The first benefit of speaking in tongues is that it gives you the assurance that you've been baptized in the Holy Spirit. In my meetings, I often urge the congregation to ask the people sitting next to them if they are saved and filled with the Spirit.

Sometimes I will even tell the congregation to ask the person beside them to pray in tongues out loud. If people are filled with the Holy Spirit, tongues will flow right out of them. If they're not filled with the Spirit, I will call them forward to receive the baptism in the Holy Spirit. I call that going fishing!

2. Tongues Will Make You Strong

Another scriptural reason for praying in tongues is that it makes your spirit strong. In First Corinthians 14:4 (NKJV), Paul wrote, "He who speaks in a tongue *edifies* himself...." The word "edify" means *to make strong*. Praying in tongues helps you become spiritually fit so you can carry out the works of God in the earth. If you have a weak, wimpy spirit, it's possible you're not praying in tongues enough.

Several years ago, there was a popular commercial on American television about Hefty trash bags. The two brands of trash bags they compared were either "wimpy, wimpy, wimpy" or "hefty, hefty, hefty."

Praying in tongues helps you become spiritually fit so you can carry out the works of God in the earth.

That's a good picture of the two types of spiritual container we can be — wimpy or hefty. And each one of us is responsible for the kind of container we are! It's our choice — will we be a wimpy container of the Holy Spirit or a hefty, "three-ply" vessel of glory?

I want to be the second category of Holy Ghost container so I can hold a great overflow of God's mighty power!

3. Tongues Will Make You Spiritually Sensitive

Praying in tongues helps you become aware of spiritual events and occurrences. It helps you increase your sensitivity to the working of the Holy Spirit. On the other hand, if you don't pray in tongues much, you won't be as sharp as you could be in your discerning of the move of the Holy Spirit or the overall unfolding of God's strategic plans.

If you don't pray in tongues much, you won't be as sharp as you could be in your discerning of the move of the Holy Spirit or the overall unfolding of God's strategic plans.

---

4. Tongues Will Build Your Faith

In Jude 20, we find that speaking in tongues stirs up and strengthens faith. Jude wrote, "But you, beloved, building yourselves up on your, most holy faith, praying in the Holy Spirit" (Jude 1:20 NKJV). Speaking in tongues makes your faith come alive! When you get through praying in tongues, you're ready to believe God for anything! It stimulates your ability to trust Him.

5. Tongues Help Clean Up Your Mouth

Praying in the Spirit helps you control the wildest member of your body — your tongue! Your tongue does more than just taste ice cream — it brings life or death, blessing or cursing, depending on how you use it (*see* Prov. 18:21).

One of the signs of Christian maturity is how much control you have over the conduct of your mouth. When you pray in tongues a lot, it makes it easier to keep your mouth in subjection to the Holy Spirit. In other words, it helps you break the unruliness of your tongue and clean up your foul talk.

I know most Christians don't cuss, but bad confessions and unbelief come out of everyone's mouth from time to time — and, according to Scripture, unbelief is just as bad as cussing. When you pray in tongues regularly, gossip and accusation begin to disappear from your speech, and holiness begins to permeate your words and actions.

James 1:26 says, "If any man among you seem to be religious [or spiritual] and bridleth not his tongue, but deceiveth his own heart, this man's religion is vain." Likewise, in James 3:8, we read, "But the tongue can no man tame; it is unruly evil, full of deadly poison."

If you are always telling people things you shouldn't be telling them, you're not yielding your mouth enough to the Lord. Praying in tongues will help you develop an awareness of the conduct of your mouth. If there was no other benefit to praying in tongues other than keeping your tongue under control, that would be reason enough to do it.

Praying in tongues will help you develop an awareness of the conduct of your mouth.

---

6. Tongues Bring Spiritual Refreshing

In Isaiah 28, we see that speaking in tongues brings spiritual refreshing:

> **For with stammering lips and another tongue will he speak to this people. To whom he said, This is the rest wherewith ye may cause the weary to rest; and this is the refreshing: yet they would not hear. But the word of the Lord was unto them precept upon precept, precept upon precept; line upon line, line upon line; here a little, and there a little....**
>
> Isaiah 28:11-13

One way Christians are supposed to find their rest is by praying in tongues.

Someone once approached Smith Wigglesworth and said, "Brother Wigglesworth, don't you ever take a vacation?"

"Every day," he responded.

"What do you mean?"

"I pray in tongues daily, and I get refreshed," Wigglesworth answered. "That's my vacation; that's my holiday."

Have you ever felt like you were tired, but there was no reason to be tired? When you feel like that, you need to pray in tongues and cause that refreshing to spring up inside your spirit. Weariness and tiredness will go, and strength from the inside out will come to you. And as you are faithful to pray in tongues every day, you will help keep yourself continually invigorated and refreshed.

> **As you are faithful to pray in tongues every day, you will help keep yourself continually invigorated and refreshed.**

7. Tongues Give You Power To Be a Witness

Another benefit of tongues is that it gives you power to be a witness.

> **But you shall receive power when the Holy Spirit has come upon you, and you shall be witnesses to Me in Jerusalem, and in all Judea and Samaria, and to the end of the earth.**
>
> **Acts 1:8 NKJV**

Consider the transformation of the disciples after the Holy Spirit's outpouring on the Day of Pentecost (*see* Acts 2). These men — who formerly had denied Jesus, feared the masses, and fought among themselves about who would be the greatest — were suddenly preaching with such boldness that the Bible says they would go on to turn the world upside down (*see* Acts 17:6)! After Peter preached on the Day of Pentecost, 3,000 souls were added to the Church that very day (*see* Acts 2:41)! That's powerful witnessing!

Jesus said tongues would play a major role in the Great Commission, and indeed they did for the Early Church:

> **And He said to them, "Go into all the world and preach the gospel to every creature. He who believes and is baptized will be saved; but he who does not believe will be**

condemned. And these signs will follow those who believe: In My name they will cast out demons; they will speak with new tongues."

Mark 16:15-17 NKJV

A lot of people think that the Great Commission ends with Jesus' words: "…Go into all the world and preach…." But He continued in verse 17, saying, *"…They will speak with new tongues."*

Speaking in the Languages of the Earth

Many conservative Christians say speaking in new tongues means supernaturally receiving the ability to speak in a foreign language known to man. I can see why they would say that.

On the Day of Pentecost, during the Azusa Street outpouring of 1906, and even at times in this day we live in, God has given some the ability to supernaturally speak the natural languages of the earth with fluency for His purposes. This is one aspect of the baptism of the Holy Spirit our generation needs to be open to. God will sometimes grant this type of manifestation with those baptized in the Holy Spirit.

I remember hearing these kinds of stories from my grandmother and others who were part of early Pentecostalism. When some received the baptism in the Holy Spirit, they began to miraculously speak in a foreign language.

In 1901 in Topeka, Kansas, a minister named Charles Parham began to receive the understanding of what it means to be baptized in the Holy Spirit. A woman by the name of Agnes Ozman was the first to receive the baptism in the Holy Spirit under Parham's ministry.[1] When Agnes received her prayer language, she received the ability not only to speak a perfect Chinese dialect, but also to *write* it.

This was documented at the time by the United States government. They sent language specialists to Topeka to investigate the outbreak of this phenomena. When the government workers got there, they recorded 20 different discernible languages being spoken, as well as a language they could not interpret. Just as this happened in the early days of the Pentecostal movement, I believe this type of manifestation will begin to happen more and more in the days ahead.

People also experienced this during the Azusa Street outpouring. Missionaries from Azusa Street were sent to almost every major people group in the world. They believed that whatever earthly language they spoke when they were filled with the Holy Spirit indicated where they were called to go and preach. If they spoke in an African-sounding dialect, they bought a boat ticket and floated over to Africa. When they got off the boat, they spoke their language until somebody understood them, and then they just went right on preaching.

Some went to China. When they got off the boat and started praying in tongues, their language would activate, and the people would start responding! Now that's a call! And that's the way it worked for many of them. Others were able to speak in a foreign language only periodically, and when they got to their mission field, they had to learn the language themselves. Why it worked for some and not others, I don't know, but I do believe that when Jesus said, "...They shall speak with new tongues"

---

[1] Vinson Synan, PhD, "The Origins of the Pentecostal Movement," *The Holy Spirit Research Center* (Oral Roberts University); http://webapps.oru.edu/new_php/library/holyspirit/pentorg1.html.

(Mark 16:17), it included the natural languages of the earth as well as the spiritual languages of Heaven. These two types of language work together.

This is why the Azusa Street outpouring spread so rapidly throughout the earth. Believers who had received the baptism of the Holy Spirit understood the importance of their prayer language in the role of world evangelism. Speaking in tongues gave them power to be effective witnesses for Christ!

Chapter 7

Your Prayer Language Should Grow

> And they were all filled with the Holy Spirit and began to speak with other tongues, as the Spirit gave them utterance.
>
> **Acts 2:4 NKJV**

Notice here that it says the disciples "...*began* to speak with other tongues." The phrase "began to speak" indicates this was *not* a onetime occurrence; the practice of speaking in tongues continued in their lives and ministries and did not cease after the Day of Pentecost.

When some people first begin to speak in tongues, they don't have fluency or a large spiritual vocabulary. They are like little children who talk in single words or broken phrases when they're first learning how to speak. When some believers are first filled with the Spirit, they may have only one word they can utter in tongues, so they just say it over and over. But that's okay. It's all part of growing and maturing spiritually.

Your prayer language should grow. Greater utterance should come up from your spirit as the Spirit of God gives you greater fluency.

God gave the prophet Isaiah a glimpse of tongues in their infancy.

> **For with stammering lips and another tongue he will speak to this people, to whom He said, "This is the rest with which you may cause the weary to rest," and, "This is the refreshing"; yet they would not hear.**
>
> **Isaiah 28:11-12 NKJV**

When Isaiah used the words "stammering lips," he was prophetically referring to Spirit-filled believers who are not quite fluent in the language of the Spirit yet. Have you ever seen Christians who pray like that? They have no fluency in their prayer language; they just mutter. Some Christians have been filled with the Holy Spirit for 20 years, but when they speak in tongues, they're still saying the equivalent of, "See Jane run. Spot jumped over the ball."

**Your prayer language should grow.
Greater utterance should come up from your spirit
as the Spirit of God gives you greater fluency.**

Your Prayer Language Should Grow

To me, that's really sad. Our tongues are supposed to grow as a language. Stammering lips are supposed to give way to stronger and deeper utterances.

How To Develop Fluency

If you've heard someone speak in broken English, you have an idea of what some Christians sound like when they pray in the Spirit. There's no fluency. It's a beginning, but they're not really speaking a language yet; it's just stammering lips. It's like a baby learning to say "*mama*" and "*dada.*"

If you're not as fluent in tongues as you should be, realize this: The way that a little child learns his native language is the same way you're going to learn to pray more fluently in the Spirit. Your tongues will grow as you keep using them. Just keep praying in the heavenly language you have until the utterance becomes more and more distinct and clear. As you learn how to yield, your language in tongues will mature, and it won't take years. God will give you more and more variety of articulation.

Your tongues will grow as you keep using them. Just keep praying in the heavenly language you have until the utterance becomes more and more distinct and clear.

The way it works in the natural for children learning a new language is the same way it works in the Spirit realm. The only difference is that *it doesn't take as long* when you engage in purposeful development and the deliberate exercising of this gift of tongues. Just do as Paul told Timothy to do: "...Stir up the gift of God..." (2 Tim. 1:6). That means you must *exercise* and *use* that gift.

It's Time To Expand Your Prayer Language

If you have been baptized in the Holy Spirit for years and your tongues are still limited to a few basic utterances or syllables, it's time to grow. I want to encourage you to begin to press into the Holy Spirit and allow Him to expand your prayer language.

Begin to speak in the tongues you have, but when Holy Spirit utterance begins to bubble up from your spirit that isn't quite what you're used to, go ahead and speak it out. Don't let your mind talk you out of releasing those unfamiliar sounds and syllables.

I want to encourage you to begin to press into the Holy Spirit and allow Him to expand your prayer language.

Don't assume speaking rapidly in tongues is anointed either. You'll pray rapidly at times, but there will be other times that you'll be led by the Holy Spirit to pray more slowly. That often happens to me right before the Holy Spirit leads me into groanings and travailings (which I'll talk about more later) or when I'm picking something up in my spirit. That may not happen to you, but that's what happens to me. It's different for everyone.

Your Prayer Language Should Grow

You can become the most fluent "tongues-talker" in the Body of Christ if you want to. It's available to whomever will pursue that goal. All you need to do is exercise the gift you've been given by praying much in the Holy Ghost!

If you aren't quite fluent in tongues yet, just lift your hands right now and begin to pray in the tongues you have. Reach out to God, and He will help you increase in the free flow of your personal prayer language.

Chapter 8

Tongues Help Our Infirmities

> **Likewise the Spirit also helpeth our infirmities: for we know not what we should pray for as we ought: but the Spirit itself maketh intercession for us with groanings which cannot be uttered. And he that searcheth the hearts knoweth what is the mind of the Spirit, because he maketh intercession for the saints according to the will of God.**
>
> **Romans 8:26-27**

Notice what Romans 8:26 says: "Likewise the Spirit also helpeth our infirmities...." Of all the great verses of the Bible, this is one that every Christian needs to get a revelation of!

If you can get these two verses to come alive inside you, *nothing* will be impossible for you to overcome — *no matter how bad it looks in the natural.* It doesn't matter if you are facing the death sentence or if the Mafia, the FBI, and the IRS are all after you — this one revelation will bring you through to victory!

When we see the word "infirmities" in verse 26, most people only think of sickness or disease. Those are major infirmities — but there are other types of infirmities as well. That word in the Greek can mean *any time you are struggling or feel inadequate to deal with a situation, whether it's physically, mentally, or emotionally.* For instance, you may face a crisis with your children, with your finances, with a neighbor or a business associate, or in your marriage. These are all types of infirmities.

That's why God inspired Paul to write, "Likewise the Holy Spirit also helpeth our infirmities…" (Rom. 8:26). What does the Holy Spirit help us do with our infirmities? He comes to help us *get rid of them,* not build a Holiday Inn for them!

A Christian's Number-One 'Infirmity'

I had the privilege of knowing Dr. John G. Lake's daughter and son-in-law, Gertrude and Wilford Reidt, before they passed away. They were good friends of mine.

Once I heard the Reidts preach in Los Angeles at a meeting called "Secrets of Intercession." Wilford was on the platform just talking a bit to the congregation, when all of a sudden he began to speak with a fresh authority. He said, "The main infirmity of the Church is not sickness or the lack of money. The main infirmity of the Church is *ignorance.*"

Tongues Help Our Infirmities

What a truthful statement! One of the greatest infirmities in the Body of Christ is not that we don't have a will to do what is right — it's that we don't know what to do!

Even if you're a seasoned Bible student and you're faithful to set aside daily time with the Lord, you'll still experience situations in life when you don't know what to do. You may know four or five scriptures that could apply to the situation. The question is, which one will turn your infirmity into a victorious situation and bless everyone involved?

For instance, Proverbs 18:22 says, "Whoso findeth a wife findeth a good thing...." But when a man doesn't know *who* and *how* and *when* to apply that scripture to his own life, that's an infirmity!

It's an infirmity to not know which direction to turn or which scripture to apply to a specific situation. It is an infirmity to not know the specific will of God in a matter. But the Holy Spirit helps you with that kind of infirmity. For instance, He may highlight a verse that applies to the situation you are facing, making it come alive to you.

It is an infirmity to not know the specific will of God in a matter. But the Holy Spirit helps you with that kind of infirmity.

When the Holy Spirit illuminates a scripture to a person, it becomes a specific word from God. Sometimes I hear people say, "That scripture jumped off the page at me!" I don't normally look for "glowing scriptures" for my guidance, but if one ever does glow, I'll receive it!

Praying About Major Decisions

Praying in tongues helps make your spirit sensitive to the Holy Spirit when He is communicating with you. It also helps you accurately express before God the inquiring of your spirit as you seek Him. And in those times of praying in the Spirit and seeking the Lord, He likes to respond to you in specifics.

For instance, it's nice to know it's God's will for you to own a home, but are you buying the right one? When you're investing $150,000 or more, you have to know what you're getting into. It's not like buying a piece of bubble gum! Once you sign your name on that loan, you're going to spend 30, 40, or maybe even 50 years paying off that mortgage. You don't want to be in a house that's not right for you. Praying much in tongues will help you develop a sensitivity so that when you walk up the driveway, you'll be sensitive enough to hear God say, *"No, don't buy it,"* or *"Yes, it's for you!"*

In that phrase, "the Spirit helpeth our infirmities" (Rom. 8:26), that word "infirmities" is plural. That means the Holy Spirit helps us with *all* of our infirmities, not just one or two of them. He helps us in every area of life — physically, mentally, and spiritually.

When you're making major decisions in life, always inquire of the Lord. Ask Him in your native language, and then pray in tongues to take care of the specifics.

Tongues Help Our Infirmities

The Holy Spirit helps us with *all* of our infirmities, not just one or two of them. He helps us in every area of life — physically, mentally, and spiritually.

If you don't get a good solid "Yes," just keep praying in tongues and praying with your understanding until you get a direct answer. You won't make bad decisions that way. God doesn't want you to make bad decisions; He wants you to make *wise* decisions.

Now, don't go overboard with what I'm saying. Sometimes people think they have to ask God about everything.

For instance, you don't need to ask, "Lord, is it okay for me to have some bubble gum?" or, "What flavor should I buy today?" Buy whatever flavor of gum makes your tastebuds jump and enjoy it!

You also don't need to ask, "God, am I supposed to eat lunch today?" Of course He wants you to eat lunch. That's why He made fruits, vegetables, and cows — so you can eat them!

Don't bother God with questions like that. That's religious. God made food for you to enjoy! And if God told you to fast today, you don't need to ask Him about eating lunch in that situation either — because He's already told you what to do!

Praying for Things Your Mind Doesn't Know To Pray For

Romans 8:26 tells us, "Likewise the Spirit also helpeth our infirmities: for we know not what we should pray as we ought."

God gave you tongues because you don't always know how to pray the right way. Sometimes when you're praying in tongues, the Holy Spirit will lead you to pray for something your mind never thought to pray for. Or sometimes He will have you pray for something that you thought you had already prayed through. All of a sudden, the Spirit of God will boil up from inside you and move you to pray about something you were not expecting.

God gave you tongues because you don't always know how to pray the right way.

The Holy Spirit knows the future, and sometimes He'll move you to pray in order to stop something tragic from happening to you. He also knows when you will experience a great deal of bombardment because of your calling, so He will prompt you to pray to make sure you won't be touched, bothered, or distracted when you walk through the fray.

The Holy Spirit strengthens you in your inner man so you'll be prepared for the attack and keep right on going. The hardship won't be able to stop or distract you.

Words in Your Native Language

Sometimes when you're praying in tongues, words in your native language will rise up from your spirit man. That's the Holy Spirit helping your mind to be edified while you're in prayer.

The key is to yield to the Holy Spirit when you pray and learn to follow His leading. The apostle Paul talked about this in 1 Corinthians 14:13-15 (NKJV):

> **Therefore let him who speaks in a tongue pray that he may interpret. For if I pray in a tongue, my spirit prays, but my understanding is unfruitful. What is the conclusion then? I will pray with the spirit, and I will also pray with the understanding. I will sing with the spirit, and I will also sing with the understanding.**

The key is to yield to the Holy Spirit when you pray and learn to follow His leading.

When I pray in tongues, many times words in English will come to me — sometimes just a word or two, sometimes more. I just obey the Holy Spirit and pray out the words that rise up from my spirit, and then I go right back into praying in tongues.

What I speak out in English is often the interpretation of what I am praying in the Spirit, but it could also be something different. No hard-and-fast rules exist when it comes to the wonderful world of tongues. I try never to declare that certain ways of doing things are unchanging laws of working with the

Holy Spirit — because as soon as I do, He will do something different!

When you're praying on behalf of another, you often won't know what you're praying about. You'll just have to trust God and make yourself available to be used as an intercessor. In those situations, you won't know what you prayed for until you get to Heaven.

The Holy Spirit works mainly by the power of words. Things move, appear, and disappear when the words you pray are inspired by the Spirit of God.

When God speaks through you and says, "No!" — things will disappear. When God speaks through you and says, "Yes!" — things will begin to show up!

The Holy Spirit works mainly by the power of words. Things move, appear, and disappear when the words you pray are inspired by the Spirit of God.

'Why Am I Praying This?'

Have you ever been praying for your spouse or family members and thought, *Why am I praying this?* That's the Holy Spirit helping you pray! I've contended in prayer over my ministry and thought, *We're in peace right now. Nothing bad is happening. Why am I praying like this?* But suddenly it just came up in my spirit. I've learned by experience that if I don't yield to the

Holy Spirit's unction to pray in situations like that, there will come a day when I wish I had!

If you wait until the battle begins in the natural, you'll have to fight with your soulish reactions as well as with the situation. I'll tell you from experience — that's hard work!

It's good to get your prayer work accomplished before you actually step into a major situation. That's why I always encourage people to pray *much* before they go on a mission trip. That way when they get there, the spiritual work is almost complete, except for the little bit that needs to be done while they're there. They just walk through the trip and have fun.

Years ago we did this before our annual camp meetings. We prayed and we prayed and we prayed! By the time we got to the first service, we just jumped into the meeting without a lot of work, and we enjoyed the blessings of God.

It's good to get your prayer work accomplished before you actually step into a major situation.

PRAYING THE PERFECT WILL OF GOD

When we don't know how to pray, we can always trust the Holy Spirit to pray through us in tongues and in our native language. He knows exactly what needs to be done, and He will help us pray according to the perfect will of God.

At times, people come up to me and ask me to pray with them. I don't know their situation, but I want God to help them, so I pray, "Father, I lift them before You in Jesus' Name"; then I just let the Holy Spirit pray through me in tongues. As I do, I know I'm praying correctly for the situation.

We are affected emotionally when we go through tragedy, but our emotions don't do a lot to move God. *Faith* moves Him.

Praying in your natural language won't always be enough to solve the problem either. Your human vocabulary doesn't contain enough words to adequately pray for the situation. You need to get to a place where you can focus and begin to let the Holy Spirit pray through you in tongues.

Always remember that you are not praying to get through to God. You're allowing the Holy Spirit to pray through you for the purpose of effecting a change in the heavens and in the natural realm.

THE DEVIL IS THE SOURCE OF YOUR TROUBLE

In the latter half of Romans 8:26, it says, "...But the Spirit itself maketh intercession for us...." This should really read, "but the Spirit *Himself*," because the Holy Spirit is not an *it* — He is a *Person*.

You know from Scripture that Jesus in His present-day ministry sits at the right hand of the Father in Heaven, ever making intercession for you (*see* Heb. 7:25). But you also need to know that the Holy Spirit will pray for you when there is no one else on this earth to pray for you. You are never without prayer. Sometimes He'll pray all by Himself, and sometimes He'll pray

Tongues Help Our Infirmities

through someone who is concerned for you — but most of the time, the Spirit of God will pray through *you*.

Some people think the Holy Spirit's only job is to give you comfort in the midst of your infirmities. He does that, but the main comfort He brings is deliverance *out* of your trouble! The Holy Spirit wants to give you knowledge that will solve your problem. He comes to show you a way of escape. He shows you what to do and say in precarious situations. He makes power available to kill the disease that is tormenting your body.

"But, Brother Roberts, I think God gave me this trouble to teach me something."

Get it straight in your head right now — *the DEVIL is the source of everything evil in your life.* All trouble originates from his malignant mind.

**The Holy Spirit wants to give you knowledge that will solve your problem.
He comes to show you a way of escape.**

The devil will do anything he can to keep you in bondage. He will even quote you the words of an old religious song! Religious spirits will try to murder you while you're singing "Amazing Grace"!

On the other hand, the Bible declares boldly that "every good gift and every perfect gift is from above, and comes down from the Father of lights, with whom there is no variation or shadow of turning" (James 1:17 NKJV). God says, *"I've come to help you get free. I've come to deliver you. I've come to give you help in a time of need."*

Pray in Tongues When You're Tired

To be truthful, even though I know that is what God is always ready to say to me, at times I've felt like saying to *Him*, "Lord, I've prayed the prayer of faith. I've bound; I've loosed; I've submitted; I've sung; I've done cartwheels across the lawn in front of my house. I've prayed every kind of prayer available, and yet this stronghold is still laughing at me and punching me in the nose! Hello, are You there, God? Has all of Heaven gone to bed?"

Have you ever felt like that? Thank God, there's a prayer that solves all these problems. When I feel that way, I'm so glad I have been empowered by the Holy Spirit! I'm so glad He lives big inside me! My help is not in my biceps; *it's in the Spirit.* All I have to do is just open my mouth and allow the Holy Spirit to pray through me in tongues, and eventually those stubborn strongholds will yield to His power that comes on the scene as I pray out the perfect will of God!

Sometimes storms hit you when you're not expecting them, and your mind doesn't just react — it faints. You get really grumpy, and you don't want to think much. You don't believe anything, and you don't even want to read the Bible. I've been there; I know what it's like.

It doesn't matter how strong you are or how long you've been walking with God — at times the storms of life will be so overwhelming that your mind will faint. At times, in the natural, you won't be able to get yourself together enough to pray by your understanding. But the Spirit of God will bubble up inside you when your soul has fainted, and He will help you pray.

All I have to do is just open my mouth and allow the Holy Spirit to pray through me in tongues, and eventually those stubborn strongholds will yield to His power that comes on the scene as I pray out the perfect will of God!

Thank God for the gift of unknown tongues! When your mind faints, tongues will flow right out of your belly and begin working to strengthen you and change the situation.

The Devil's Multiple Warheads

At times in my life, I have experienced what I call "multiple warheads." In other words, when the devil can't get me with just one bomb anymore, he comes at me in multiples.

Have you ever experienced those kinds of attacks? After winning the victory in a few heated battles, you'll become a veteran in war and the devil's attacks won't bother you as much.

I'm immune to most of the enemy's strategies. It doesn't bother me when people want to fight with me. I've been through money wars, rumor wars, and spirit wars — I've been through every kind of war you can think of. These kinds of attacks don't bother me anymore. When a new attack comes at me, I just say, "Get a number and get in line! Next!"

The first few times I went through a war, it was a big deal. But after the third or fourth time, it didn't register anymore. I just went out and enjoyed a delightful meal.

After winning the victory in a few heated battles, you'll become a veteran in war and the devil's attacks won't bother you as much.

Perhaps you're facing some major battles right now, and you're not at the place yet where you can respond to an attack like that.

- What happens when you're in trouble and no one is around at midnight to help you?

- What happens when the one you're calling doesn't give you that word of encouragement you're looking for to get you through another hour?

- What happens when those who call you on the phone only give you more bad reports?

- What happens when your troubled soul constantly reminds you of the pain you're in and not the peace you should have?

- What happens when your friends or family members try to help you out, but they unknowingly cooperate with the negative atmosphere and pressures of the attack that's being waged against you?

Tongues Help Our Infirmities

I've been in the midst of difficult times when people tried the best they knew how to encourage me, but they just couldn't do it.

But that's why you have the wonderful world of tongues! When your soul faints during a crisis or time of need, the Holy Spirit rises within you to strengthen you, comfort you, and assist you in prayer. All you have to do is yield to Him and let Him take charge. He will pull you through!

When your soul faints during a crisis or time of need, the Holy Spirit rises within you to strengthen you, comfort you, and assist you in prayer.

It would be nice if God came down and by His sovereignty fixed our problems — and sometimes He does. But most of the time the Holy Spirit takes hold together with us and helps God's will to prevail in the situation through the wonderful world of tongues.

Chapter 9

The Gift of Tongues and the Gift of Interpretation of Tongues

> But the manifestation of the Spirit is given to every man to profit withal. For to one is given by the Spirit the word of wisdom; to another the word of knowledge by the same Spirit; to another faith by the same Spirit; to another the gifts of healing by the same Spirit; to another the working of miracles; to another prophecy; to another discerning of spirits; to another divers kinds of tongues; to another the interpretation of tongues: but all these worketh that one and the selfsame Spirit, dividing to every man severally as he will.
>
> 1 Corinthians 12:7-11

In this passage of Scripture, the apostle Paul lists nine separate gifts of the Spirit. Two of these nine gifts, the gift of diverse kinds of tongues and the gift of interpretation of tongues, are "married" in that they function as one. One can't manifest without the other.

When someone gives a message in tongues in the congregation, an interpretation should always accompany it. When these two gifts of the Spirit manifest together, they perform the same function as the gift of prophecy — to edify, exhort, and to comfort (see 1 Cor. 14:3). The gift of tongues, the gift of the interpretation of tongues, and the gift of prophecy are all gifts that God uses to communicate to people. They are known as the "utterance gifts."

Tongues for Public Assembly

The gifts of tongues and the interpretation of tongues often manifest in a church service without warning. The unction to operate in these gifts may come upon the pastor, a pastoral team member, or someone in the congregation. Suddenly the gift of tongues will manifest in a language that is unknown to those in the room; then the interpretation to that message in tongues will follow.

If you are discerning in the Spirit, you'll sense when these gifts are present in a meeting. However, just because you're sensing a "tongue" doesn't mean you're supposed to give it. If you don't have an unction, just remain still. When the unction comes on you, you'll have a strong knowing. It will feel as if it's boiling up from within you, like water boiling on the stove.

The Gift of Tongues and the Gift of Interpretation of Tongues

Everything will be really calm in the pot, but as the heat gets hotter, it will bubble up and overflow.

An unction will just keep coming up in you stronger and stronger until it seems like you just can't hold it back anymore. As you yield to the Holy Spirit — boom! — that utterance will suddenly come out of your mouth, and sometimes you will be the most surprised person in the room! You may think, *Oh, my, what did I do? Did I do something wrong?* No, you were just used by God to manifest the gift of tongues.

It is then time for all who are present to wait for someone to give the interpretation. Everyone may wait for a few minutes; then suddenly someone will give the interpretation. The one giving the interpretation may be the same person who gave the message in tongues — or it could be someone on the other side of the room. It will not be a word-for-word translation of what the person said in tongues, but the interpretation will capture the gist of the Holy Spirit's message.

When a public tongue comes like that, an interpretation must follow every time so everyone in the room can understand (*see* 1 Cor. 14:27-28). If a sinner is sitting in the congregation, he should not be left wondering to himself, *What in the world was that?*

What If There's No Interpretation?

As I mentioned, the gifts of tongues and the interpretation of tongues together equal the gift of prophecy. When someone flows in the gift of prophecy, there is no need of tongues. Prophecy is a divine utterance in the native language of the people that is spoken forth so the congregation can be edified and the church built up.

In the same way, God also uses the gifts of tongues and the interpretation of tongues to communicate to His people — to encourage them, to comfort them, to correct them, and to admonish them. So whenever a public tongue is released, it should always be accompanied by an interpretation.

"But Brother Roberts, what if someone doesn't give the interpretation? What do we do?"

You just go on with the service. But ten times out of ten, if it's a true message in tongues, an interpretation is in the room somewhere. If the interpretation doesn't come, it might be because the person who received the interpretation is scared to give it and is holding back. That person may keep pushing down the unction to speak out the interpretation, which grieves the Spirit of God. When that happens, the Holy Spirit will move on someone else to give the interpretation. That's why it sometimes takes awhile for the interpretation to come forth after a message in tongues is given.

**God uses the gifts of tongues
and the interpretation of tongues to communicate
to His people — to encourage them, to comfort them,
to correct them, and to admonish them.**

It's different when a congregation is spiritually fluent and moves in the gifts with no fear or embarrassment. In that case, when a message in tongues comes, the interpretation will come

The Gift of Tongues and the Gift of Interpretation of Tongues

almost before the tongue is finished. The Holy Spirit will move on someone, and that person will just start bubbling over with the interpretation to the tongues.

LEADERSHIP CAN USUALLY INTERPRET

When no interpretation comes from the congregation, someone in the leadership can usually receive it if he or she will ask the Holy Spirit for it.

As a minister, I can usually get the interpretation of a tongue, whether or not I sense the unction to give it. I usually receive the gist of it, and many times I receive the interpretation word for word. But if I interpreted all the time, people in the congregation would never do it; they'd just wait for me to give the interpretation. That's why I don't usually step out and immediately interpret when a public message in tongues is spoken.

Sometimes a series of tongues and interpretations will come, one after the other. Some may ask, "Why can't God say everything all at once?" The answer is a simple one — because He doesn't want to.

It's similar to what happens when I'm overseas preaching in a nation that speaks a different language than I do. When I get up and say, "How is everybody doing?" — the interpreter translates my short sentence and then waits for me to give the next one. The interpreter has to break down my sermon into little sections to ensure he or she speaks out what I say accurately to the people. The Holy Spirit often does the same thing when He's communicating to His people through the gifts of tongues and interpretation.

Don't Be Afraid To Flow

When you're being used in the gift of tongues and interpretation, don't let your mind talk you out of what you're hearing in your spirit. Sometimes your mind will say, *Everyone thinks you're crazy! They're not receiving what you're saying! You're missing it!* When that happens, you have to tell your mind to be still. You have to quiet your mind so your spirit has the freedom to do what it needs to do.

Over the years, I have seen the Spirit of God fall on certain ones at certain times, but they're too afraid of making a mistake to speak it out. I can almost hear them thinking, *What if I'm not right?*

When you're being used in the gift of tongues and interpretation, don't let your mind talk you out of what you're hearing in your spirit. You have to quiet your mind so your spirit has the freedom to do what it needs to do.

If your tongue or interpretation is not quite right, a leader who is led by the Holy Spirit won't embarrass you! If that happened in a service where I was ministering, I would help you out a little if necessary, or I'd just let the Spirit of God make the adjustments. God can take care of things without my help, and He does a much better job than I ever could. If the Spirit of God boils up in you during a meeting and gives you a tongue and an interpretation, have the courage to just go ahead and yield to what He is giving you the unction to do.

The Gift of Tongues and the Gift of Interpretation of Tongues

"Is there any special time to give it?"

Yes, when He comes on you to give it.

"What if the minister is in the middle of his sermon?"

If I'm preaching and it's truly the Holy Spirit who is moving on someone to release a message in tongues and interpretation, the interruption doesn't bother me at all. I'll just be quiet for a moment and let the Holy Spirit speak to the people directly instead of through me.

If the Spirit of God boils up in you during a meeting and gives you a tongue and an interpretation, have the courage to just go ahead and yield to what He is giving you the unction to do.

Normally, however, if the Holy Spirit is allowed to flow in your church, you will sense the timing of when He wants to move in this way in a service. Sadly, many churches today don't experience the blessing of the utterance gifts because they don't make time for them to manifest during their services.

'Won't They Think We're Crazy?'

"But, Brother Roberts, if unbelievers come into the church and hear someone speaking in tongues, won't they think we're crazy?" No, as First Corinthians 14:22 says, "Wherefore tongues are a sign, not to them that believe, but to them that believe not...." Tongues are a sign to those who aren't saved, as well as to those who haven't yet received the fullness of the Holy Spirit.

Some churches are embarrassed by the gifts of tongues and the interpretation of tongues, so they push them over into a corner. But pastors should never be afraid that tongues and interpretation will spook their unsaved visitors. Tongues are a sign to those visitors! And the truth is, the people who get upset about tongues in the assembly are generally *Christians*, not sinners!

It's true that there are times when the gifts of tongues and interpretation should not be in the forefront during a service. However, neither the pastor nor his congregation should ever be embarrassed about these gifts.

In First Corinthians 14:39 (NKJV), Paul wrote, "Therefore, brethren, desire earnestly to prophesy, and do not forbid to speak with tongues." Earlier in that chapter, Paul also wrote, "I thank my God I speak with tongues more than you all" (v. 18 NKJV). As we saw earlier, that means Paul prayed in tongues a great deal — and he was not ashamed of it.

Tongues are a sign to nonbelievers. Tongues will encourage them, inspire them, and increase their awareness of God.

CHAPTER 10

Interpreting Your Personal Prayer Language

In First Corinthians 14:13, Paul wrote: "Wherefore let him that speaketh in an unknown tongue pray that he may interpret." This verse does not pertain to the gifts of tongues and interpretation of tongues for public assembly. Instead, the apostle Paul was writing here about interpreting your own personal prayer language.

You receive an interpretation of your personal prayer language the same way you receive an interpretation of tongues in a public setting — through the operation of the gift of interpretation of tongues. The first thing you have to do is make time for the interpretation to come back to you when you're praying in tongues.

Some people have never had their prayer language interpreted back to them by the Holy Spirit simply because they never took this first step. They have never made time for the interpretation to come. Others may simply be "in training." In other words, they may still be learning how to discern the voice of the Holy Spirit in their own spirit when He wants to give them the interpretation of what they are praying in tongues.

When the Spirit of God does give you the interpretation, He may speak to you in great detail about what you've been praying about, or He may just let you know the gist of it. At times, an interpretation will be available, but if you don't give time in prayer to receive it, it won't come.

Some people have never had their prayer language interpreted back to them by the Holy Spirit simply because they have never made time for the interpretation to come.

Sometimes while I'm praying in tongues, I instantly understand what I'm saying. You may have had that happen to you, but you didn't know what it was. It may have seemed like your mind was recalling specific scriptures, and it just didn't occur to you that it was actually the Holy Spirit interpreting your prayer language.

Oral Roberts' Explanation of How He Built ORU

Oral Roberts, the powerful, high-profile healing evangelist who blazed a trail of miracles across postwar America, related how interpreting his personal prayer language helped him build a university for the Lord in Tulsa, Oklahoma. As Oral was walking across a cow pasture one day, praying in tongues, the Lord said to him, *"Oral, I want you to buy the land you're walking on and build Me a university."*

Oral knew it was God speaking to him, but he had no idea how to build something as large as a university. So he walked back and forth across the field praying in tongues and then waiting for the interpretation. When the interpretation came, Oral would speak out in English what he had been praying in tongues.

That's how Oral knew what to do and when to do it. That's how he found out how to raise enough money to get it done. He allowed the Spirit of God to interpret back to his mind what he was communicating with God about in tongues.

Today Oral Roberts University (ORU) sits on 323 acres and has 25 major buildings — with new structures being planned. More than 61,000 students have passed through its classrooms since 1963.

INTERPRETING YOUR TONGUES HELPS YOUR MIND

Look at First Corinthians 14:14-15 (NKJV) more closely:

> **For if I pray in a tongue, my spirit prays, but my understanding is unfruitful. What is the conclusion then? I will pray with the spirit, and I will also pray with the understanding. I will sing with the spirit, and I will also sing with the understanding.**

Notice that Paul said in verse 14 (NKJV), "For if I pray in a tongue, my spirit prays, but my understanding is unfruitful." In other words, Paul was saying that when you pray in tongues, your mind does not understand what you're saying. That's why it is important that you pray every day in your native language, as well as in tongues. You should also sing every day in your native language, as well as in tongues.

Making this your daily practice helps your mind stay in touch with what is happening in your spirit. Interpreting what the Holy Spirit has been praying through you can also help you determine the true spiritual condition of your life. Your mind doesn't know what your spirit knows, so one way for your mind to become more enlightened is by listening to the interpretation of your private tongues.

Your private interpretation does not usually come like a public interpretation. Tongues and interpretation in a public assembly come boldly and are evident to all who are present. In your private prayer life, an interpretation may quietly rise up from your spirit and then enter into your mind. When you speak it out, there may or may not be an authoritative tone to it.

Your mind doesn't know what your spirit knows, so one way for your mind to become more enlightened is by listening to the interpretation of your private tongues.

There is another advantage for believers who stay open to the Holy Spirit using them to interpret their own prayer language: It helps keep their minds strong and their way of thinking correct. When people don't fill their minds with God's thoughts, their thinking can get a little off center in their pursuit of being "spiritual" and they can begin to lose touch with reality.

But there is a sure way to avoid that trap. It's a matter of renewing our minds with the Word of God, making a daily practice of praying and singing in both our native language *and* in tongues, and allowing the Holy Spirit to interpret our prayer language back to us as it pleases Him. As that becomes our way of life, our minds will *not* be unfruitful.

Chapter 11

Diversities of Tongues

> **And God hath set some in the church, first apostles, secondarily prophets, thirdly teachers, after that miracles, then gifts of healings, helps, governments,** *diversities of tongues.*
>
> 1 Corinthians 12:28

This verse contains a lineup of gifts, functions, or roles within the Body of Christ that Jesus "set" into the Church. These functions are not just for private use in your prayer closet. Jesus ordained them to be publicly manifested in the local church! He set apostles, prophets, teachers, and after that *miracles*!

Miracles belong in the church. They are not just for the mission field or the evangelistic crusade. God has *set* these gifts in the church, and people have no right to excommunicate them!

When God sets something into the church, that means He wants it to have a *residential existence*. In other words, the ministry gifts and functions listed in this verse are not just supposed to have "visitation rights." They are supposed to dwell *residentially* in our midst.

Miracles belong in the church. They are not just for the mission field or the evangelistic crusade. God has set these gifts in the church, and people have no right to excommunicate them!

"But, Brother Roberts, these things aren't in the church I go to!"

Then you're not in a church — *you're in a Christian club.*

Notice that this verse goes on to list other gifts or functions God has set in the church: "gifts of healings, helps, governments and *diversities of tongues*." The word "diversities" in this verse means *different kinds*. Paul was referring to different types of tongues that accomplish different purposes.

Someone said to me, "We have diversity of tongues in our church. We have some Russians who speak in Russian; we have some French who speak French; and we have some Hispanics who speak Spanish."

That's not what this verse is talking about at all! The phrase "diversities of tongues" here refers to the various kinds of utterances that bubble up from within your spirit by the supernatural power of God.

Diversities of Tongues

Rivers of Living Waters

Jesus made reference to the diversities of tongues when He spoke about the various rivers of the Holy Spirit that would flow from the heart of a believer.

> ...Jesus stood and cried out, saying, "If anyone thirsts, let him come to Me and drink. He who believes in Me, as the Scripture has said, out of his heart will flow rivers of living water." But this He spoke concerning the Spirit, whom those believing in Him would receive; for the Holy Spirit was not yet given, because Jesus was not yet glorified.
>
> **John 7:37-39 NKJV**

Jesus said, "...Out of his heart will flow *rivers* of living water" (v. 38 NKJV). The word "rivers" is plural, meaning *more than one river*. These rivers come from the Holy Spirit within you! They bubble up out of your spirit in various forms and in different flows of tongues as you work with the Spirit in prayer.

Various Kinds of Tongues

Most Bible teachers today only teach about one type of tongue — tongues for our personal edification. That's why most Christians are stuck in one zone when it comes to praying in tongues. They don't teach on the diversities of tongues that God makes available to His people.

Tongues for personal edification are important — but what about tongues of intercession? Diversities of tongues need to be taught in the church so people can understand what they are and how to flow in them. If believers know about the different diversities of tongues that are available to them, they can learn to step into different forms and flows of tongues as the Spirit of God leads. As they do, they will get things accomplished faster and more effectively in their prayer life.

Many Christians today don't know that diversities of tongues are available to them. Some may know it by chapter and verse, but they don't know it experientially. So when they begin to venture into the deeper things of God through praying in tongues, they draw back when they sense an unction to flow in different diversities of utterance because of fear or ignorance.

I believe this is the reason so many struggle with difficult situations and issues in their lives that never seem to get resolved. Believers don't know how to go deep enough in the Holy Spirit to find the answers to their problems.

The Holy Spirit knows what kind of utterance and expression is needed to bring you to victory. He also knows what level of intensity and authority is required in your prayer language in order to bring a change in the situation. And as you yield to the Spirit of God in prayer, various types of tongues will rise up out of your spirit to help you pray out and deal with the different challenges and circumstances of life.

> **The Holy Spirit knows what kind of utterance and expression is needed to bring you to victory. He also knows what level of intensity and authority is required in your prayer language in order to bring a change in the situation.**

Sometimes you'll be praying in your normal tongue, and then that tongue will suddenly change. When you experience that, your prayer language has just kicked into a new level of expression, or you're beginning to intercede effectively on behalf of a situation that needs to *shift* and go God's way.

Don't Tamper With How Your Tongues Come Out

When a tongue boils up inside your spirit by the Holy Spirit, don't tamper with it! If you get more intense than He is, if you speak more calmly than He does, if you weep when He is not weeping, if you rework your tongues in any way — it will affect your victory. You must allow your tongues to come out of you the way the Holy Spirit gives them to you.

You may also lose your victory if you infect your praying with your emotions, your fear of man, or your political preferences. I've learned this by experience. When I wouldn't pray out in tongues the way the Holy Spirit was leading me to pray, I'd lose my victory for a season. I may have prayed in a way that made all my preacher friends happy; I may have left with their blessing — but I didn't leave with victory in my life.

Thank God, I got delivered from that stupidity! I had to get to the place where I wanted victory in my private walk with God more than I wanted people's approval.

You will have to come to that place too! In order for the Holy Spirit to use you in the diversities of tongues, you have to be willing to allow Him to flow through you in whatever way He wants to flow.

If the Spirit of God wants you to pray boldly and strongly to change a situation, you'll have to obey. You won't be able to back off because you sense resistance in the atmosphere or because of your own fear that others will think you're weird. You'll have to want to please God more than man. You'll have to want your rebellious children living right more than you want everyone to think you're "normal"!

In order for the Holy Spirit to use you in the diversities of tongues, you have to be willing to allow Him to flow through you in whatever way He wants to flow.

Tongues Open the World of the Spirit

You have to *develop* in your ability to cooperate with the Holy Spirit when new words or even a new prayer language bubble up from your spirit. Just as your knowledge of how to speak English opens up the world that speaks English, your knowledge of how to yield to the Holy Spirit as you pray in tongues opens up the world of the Spirit to you.

When I go to Russia, I usually take an interpreter along to help me. When I arrive at the airport in Moscow, I become dependent upon my interpreter as soon as I get off the plane, because I don't know Russian.

My interpreter has the ability to get the job done, because he knows the language. Sometimes my interpreter will speak very nicely and politely to people in Russian, and at other times you'd think he was part of the Red Army about to attack! In the latter instance, I've asked my interpreter what was going on, and he would just respond, "I'm taking care of it."

Your knowledge of how to yield to the Holy Spirit as you pray in tongues opens up the world of the Spirit to you.

Sometimes my interpreter will inquire about something, and other times he will give commands. I can usually tell what he's doing by the sound of his words, but I don't know what he's actually saying.

When I am preaching with an interpreter, for the most part I ignore the interpreter and keep my eyes on the people I'm speaking to. I have to trust that my interpreter is accurately translating what I have said.

The Holy Spirit Is Our Interpreter

With this kind of help from interpreters, the whole world can be opened up to me. The same is true in the Spirit realm. In the same way that my interpreter speaks for me when I'm in Russia, the Holy Spirit speaks through me when I'm in the Spirit. I trust Him to lead me in how I pray in diversities of tongues to accomplish whatever He needs to accomplish through me.

The Holy Spirit will work the same way with *you* in the world of the Spirit. When you lean upon the Holy Spirit in your praying, diversities of tongues will come through you as He leads. At times your tone will change, as well as your utterances.

You see, the Holy Spirit speaks with a great variety of expression, just as we do. That's why monotone praying in tongues usually leads us to a dead-end street.

That kind of praying may have some effect, but its effectiveness will stay limited because you've kept your praying in tongues contained. You need to begin to allow the Spirit of God to manifest diversities of tongues through you privately — and at times publicly whenever He leads.

The Holy Spirit speaks with a great variety of expression, just as we do. That's why monotone praying in tongues usually leads us to a dead-end street.

Tongues *to* God and Tongues *With* God

I have heard some people say, "Tongues are for the purpose of speaking to God" (*see* 1 Cor. 14:2). That's true, but we've seen in First Corinthians 12:28 that there are *diversities* of tongues, which means different kinds of tongues for different purposes.

If all you do is limit your tongues to just speaking to God or building yourself up, you'll never get into the depths of what He has for you in the realm of prayer. You have to understand that when you're praying in tongues, sometimes you're *speaking to* God and sometimes you're *working with* God. When you're working with God in the Spirit, the Holy Spirit will use your prayer language to affect things in the earth according to God's plans and purposes. That's where intercessory prayer comes from.

Most Bible teachers today teach only about the kind of praying in tongues that is speaking to God. They don't know much about working *with* God.

When you're working with God in the Spirit, the Holy Spirit will use your prayer language to affect things in the earth according to God's plans and purposes.

When you pray *with* God, you're not lifting your voice and asking Him for things. You're yielding your mouth to the Holy Spirit so He can make intercession through you, either in tongues or in your native language.

SOME EXAMPLES OF PRAYING WITH GOD

When you yield to the Holy Spirit, sometimes you will experience what I call *breakthrough tongues*. James 5:16 (NKJV) says, "...The effective, *fervent* prayer of a righteous man avails much." Sometimes the Holy Spirit will boil up from our spirits in strong, fervent tongues in order to bring a breakthrough in a certain situation. Strong tongues are the spiritual battering ram the Holy Spirit uses to overthrow the strongholds of the enemy.

When you start praying in strong tongues, some Charismatics or old-time Pentecostals will get upset and say, "How dare you yell at God in tongues!"

I usually respond by saying, "Have you ever been in your prayer closet just worshiping the Lord when all of a sudden the Holy Spirit takes hold of your spirit and strong tongues rise up in you that sound like a big old bear?"

"Well, yes," they usually answer.

"Were you talking to God when you were praying like that?"

"Well, no."

"Was it the Holy Spirit praying through you?"

"Yes."

"So there you go! There are times the Holy Spirit gives us the unction to pray in strong tongues to break through an obstacle or to get something done — and we shouldn't get upset when it happens!"

Strong tongues are the spiritual battering ram the Holy Spirit uses to overthrow the strongholds of the enemy.

I want believers to understand the diversities of tongues so they can yield to them when the Holy Spirit causes different types of tongues to rise up in their spirit. He knows what is needed to get the job done. That's why sometimes I will say to people by the Spirit, "Change that tongue. You're praying in the wrong tongue to get victory in that situation."

You can't be praying in tongues of edification when you need a breakthrough. You must have something more!

So the bottom line is this: You have to be careful that you don't pray in those same old boring tongues all the time. If you constantly pray in the same monotone tongues and your utterances never fluctuate, you have a problem. Your fluency has been broken, and you're stuck in a rut.

Groanings, Travailings, and Weepings

Many times when you are praying, one type of tongue will give way to other operations of the Holy Spirit's ways of working through His people. Sometimes groanings, travailings, and weepings will begin to come up out of your spirit. These are also some of the languages of Heaven.

> Likewise the Spirit also helps in our weaknesses. For we do not know what we should pray for as we ought, but the Spirit Himself makes intercession for us with groanings which cannot be uttered.
>
> **Romans 8:26 NKJV**

> Who hath heard such a thing? who hath seen such things? Shall the earth be made to bring forth in one day? or shall a nation be born at once? for as soon as Zion travailed, she brought forth her children.
>
> **Isaiah 66:8**

> **My little children, of whom I travail in birth again until Christ be formed in you.**
>
> **Galatians 4:19**
>
> **Those who sow in tears shall reap in joy. He who continually goes forth weeping, bearing seed for sowing, shall doubtless come again with rejoicing, bringing his sheaves with him.**
>
> **Psalm 126:5-6 NKJV**

I have not heard much teaching on these kinds of manifestations of the Holy Spirit, but they are very real. As you pray in the Spirit, at times groanings, travailings, and weepings will come on you. You have probably already yielded to these languages of Heaven but didn't know what to call them.

For a long time, speaking in tongues boldly made people feel nervous. But now that speaking in tongues is becoming more acceptable, we have to get comfortable with the groanings, travailings, and weepings of the Spirit. These will come periodically as the Spirit of God leads, and we have to know how to yield to them. In these end-time days we're living in, it's become more important than ever, because the Church is supposed to birth many things into the earth in this way by the help of the Holy Spirit — all for the glory and the plan of God.

> **We have to get comfortable with the groanings, travailings, and weepings of the Spirit. These will come periodically as the Spirit of God leads, and we have to know how to yield to them.**

Chapter

Common Sense With the Use of Tongues

In this chapter, I want to give you a few thoughts on the practical side of praying in tongues, so it will be a blessing to you and not a hindrance.

First, when you're flowing in the gifts of tongues and interpretation of tongues, you have to be sensitive to those you are speaking to.

When you're flowing in the gifts of tongues and interpretation of tongues, you have to be sensitive to those you are speaking to.

At times when I have sensed a tongue arise in my spirit, I have had to prepare the people present to receive what was about to occur by explaining these two gifts of the Spirit.

In the early years of my ministry, I received an invitation to speak at a First Baptist church in Hartford, Connecticut. I asked my secretary to call them and make sure they knew I was a Full Gospel preacher and I spoke in tongues. To my surprise, they wanted me to come anyway, so I went. In the middle of one of the night meetings, I felt a tongue arise in my spirit, and because I wanted the people to receive it, I did my best to prepare them for what was coming.

"Folks, I'm from a Full Gospel background," I said. "We believe in the gifts of the Holy Spirit, and one of them is about to manifest right now. Don't be afraid; just sit back, relax, and receive."

After I gave the tongue and the interpretation, the people began shouting excitedly all over the room. They had never experienced anything like that before. When I gave the altar call, more than 150 people came forward and received the baptism in the Holy Spirit with the evidence of speaking in tongues! If I hadn't been sensitive to God and to the people, I wouldn't have experienced those wonderful results.

'Do I Have To Pray Loudly?'

People often approach me after my meetings and ask, "Do I have to pray in tongues loudly to be effective?"

"No," I tell them, "you just have to pray fervently to be effective" (*see* James 5:16).

Common Sense With the Use of Tongues

Praying strongly doesn't always mean praying loudly. I'm not against praying out loud in tongues, where others can hear you, but I'm not promoting a yelling contest either. Praying strongly means praying *fervently*, with a voice of authority. That voice of authority comes from the confidence and freedom that you operate in as a Spirit-filled believer when you know who you are and what you possess in Christ.

In my meetings, we pray out loud in tongues and have a great time, but you can't pray like that in every environment. For example, when you are in a hospital room praying for someone, you can't pray in tongues with all the force and volume you might use when you're in a believers' meeting. If you do, the hospital staff may take you to the thirteenth floor, strap a straitjacket on you, and commit you into the psych ward, saying, "We have someone who became mentally ill while visiting a patient!"

Praying strongly means praying *fervently*, with a voice of authority. That voice of authority comes from the confidence and freedom that you operate in as a Spirit-filled believer when you know who you are and what you possess in Christ.

You have to know how to function according to the environment you're in. That's not compromising; that's just being a witness for Christ who walks wisely before others.

I was taught as a child to pray audibly enough for my own ears to hear my voice. To me, that is still a good balance in most situations.

You Have To Be Relatable

Some Christians think they have to shout, jerk, and have a volcanic explosion every time they speak in tongues. But God is in the business of drawing people to Himself, not blowing them away! Always remember, the more spiritual a person is, the more relatable that person should be.

Praying in tongues and living a spiritual life shouldn't keep you from doing what is right in the natural either. In fact, it should help you do it better! If I had an employee who prayed so much in tongues that he didn't perform well in his job, I'd fire him! Something is wrong with a Christian who cannot function well in the natural world.

Christians who become super-spiritual and almost "spooky" often lose friends and end up feeling like everyone is against them. But praying in tongues and being spiritual shouldn't keep a Christian from being a good spouse, a good parent, a good child, a good employee, or a good citizen.

Some women who are married to unsaved husbands don't have it very easy. But if an unsaved husband comes home to a wife who does nothing but pray in tongues while neglecting the housework or her other responsibilities, why would he want to get saved and be like her?

Praying in tongues and living a spiritual life shouldn't keep you from doing what is right in the natural. In fact, it should help you do it better!

I've had to tell believers who do little more than pray in tongues all the time to get busy taking care of what needs to get done — chop wood, do the house chores, get a job, or just talk to people in their native language for a while. Sometimes people just need a reality check. They have to learn how to be relatable so they can be fruitful in God's Kingdom. After all, that's the main reason God gives us spiritual gifts — including the ability to pray out His will in tongues — in the first place!

**Sometimes people just need a reality check.
They have to learn how to be relatable
so they can be fruitful in God's Kingdom.**

CHAPTER 13

How To Minister the Baptism in the Holy Spirit

I want to give you seven simple steps to successfully ministering the baptism in the Holy Spirit to people with the evidence of speaking in other tongues. I also list six signs that should manifest in a person's life who has received the infilling of the Spirit.

1. **Show them in the Word that the Holy Spirit has already been poured out.**

    And suddenly there came a sound from heaven, as of a rushing mighty wind, and it filled the whole house where they were sitting. Then there appeared to them divided tongues, as of fire, and one sat upon each of them. And

> they were all filled with the Holy Spirit and began to speak with other tongues, as the Spirit gave them utterance.
>
> Acts 2-4 NKJV

The Holy Spirit was poured out on the Day of Pentecost, and this powerful gift has been available to believers ever since. Explain that we do not have to beg for the gift of the Holy Spirit but simply receive it by faith.

2. **Explain that all those who are born again are already qualified to receive the Holy Spirit.**

   Tell people they don't have to somehow clean up their lives in order to receive the promise of the Spirit. It's a free gift. All that's needed is to ask and receive (*see* Luke 11:13).

3. **Tell people to expect to receive when you lay your hands on them.**

   The gift of the baptism in the Holy Spirit is often imparted to believers through the laying on of hands.

   Before laying hands on them and praying, explain that you are not the one baptizing them in the Holy Spirit but that the Lord Jesus Christ is the Baptizer. The laying on of hands only serves as a point of contact by which the people may release their faith.

4. **Explain to people what is about to happen to them and tell them they are responsible to open their mouths in order to do the speaking.**

   The Holy Spirit will not do the speaking for those you are ministering to! The people receiving will have to open their mouths and yield to the inner unction and flow of the Holy Spirit.

5. **Assure people that they will not receive a counterfeit spirit.**

   There's a good reason you can be confident that the people you minister to will be filled with the One they are asking for. It is found in Jesus' words in Luke 11:11-13 (NKJV): "If a son asks for bread from any father among you, will he give him a stone? Or if he ask for a fish, will he give him a serpent instead of a fish? Or if he asks for an egg, will he offer him a scorpion? If you then, being evil, know how to give good gifts to your children, how much more will your heavenly Father give the Holy Spirit to those who ask Him!"

6. **Encourage them to act in faith by speaking out loud but not in their native language.**

   Don't allow people to speak anything in their native language. Tell them to open their mouths and begin to speak out loud by faith the syllables and sounds of their new personal prayer language that the Holy Spirit has given them.

7. **Don't allow a crowd of onlookers to gather around the person you are ministering to.**

   Onlookers can create distraction and confusion, which can hinder the person you are praying for from receiving the gift of the Holy Spirit.

SIGNS ACCOMPANYING THE BAPTISM IN THE HOLY SPIRIT

1. Initial sign — speaks in other tongues (*see* Acts 2:4).

2. Empowered to be an effective witness for Christ (*see* Luke 24:49; Acts 1:8).

3. Speaks the Word boldly (*see* Acts 4:31).

4. Operates in the gifts of the Spirit (*see* Acts 5:12; 19:6).

5. Overflows with praise to God (*see* Acts 10:46).

6. Demonstrates the fire of God — a yielding to His cleansing and a growing passion to pursue His ways (*see* Matt. 3:11).

CHAPTER 11

How To Receive the Holy Spirit and Speak With Tongues

And they were all filled with the Holy Spirit and began to speak with other tongues, as the Spirit gave them utterance.

Acts 2:4 NKJV

When seeking the baptism in the Holy Spirit, it's important for you to recognize that the disciples spoke in tongues "...as the Spirit gave them utterance" (Acts 2:4). That means in their spirits, they began to hear the voice of the Holy Spirit giving them utterances. They heard the utterances on the inside, but they had to *open their mouths* and *speak them out*.

The Supernatural Language: Why You Should Speak in Tongues

In the same way, in order for you to speak in your new prayer language, you have to quiet your mind so you can hear what the Holy Spirit is saying to you inwardly. And as you hear those sounds in your spirit, you must begin to speak out what the Holy Spirit is giving you.

Some people initially hear only one sound and say it over and over. That's a good start.

When you receive the baptism in the Holy Spirit, there is no need to experience great emotion, jerking, or falling down under the power of the Spirit. Although some people do have more dramatic experiences when they are filled with the Spirit, most do not.

It's actually a simple matter of faith. You ask Jesus to baptize you in the Holy Spirit by faith. You hear new words on the inside, where the Holy Spirit speaks to your spirit, and you begin to speak out those new words by faith. It's that simple.

Now that you know all the reasons why the devil doesn't want you to speak in tongues, it's time to receive the baptism in the Holy Spirit if you haven't already. Just pray the prayer below out loud, and then step out in faith and begin to speak in your new heavenly language.

Dear Lord Jesus,

I believe You are the One who baptizes with the Holy Spirit. I ask You to baptize me with the Holy Spirit now. I receive the fullness of Your precious Spirit by faith, and I will now begin to speak with other tongues. In Jesus' mighty name I pray, amen.

Signed _____

How To Receive the Holy Spirit and Speak With Tongues

If you were filled with the Spirit and are now speaking in tongues, I want to know about it. Please write me and describe your experience in getting baptized in the Holy Spirit. Please include your name, address, phone number, and e-mail address. You overcome the devil by the blood of the Lamb and *the word of your testimony* (*see* Rev. 12:11). I also want you to include any prayer requests you might have. Please send them to me so I can join with you in the powerful prayer of agreement.

Now that you're filled with the Holy Spirit, don't ever let the devil talk you out of the supernatural gift of tongues that you have received. It's time to get militant and forge forward with your life in God!

ABOUT THE AUTHOR

From a young age, Roberts Liardon was destined to become one of the most well-known Christian authors and orators of his generation. To date, he has sold more than 16 million books worldwide that have been translated into 60+ international languages. Roberts has ministered in 127 countries, both to the multitudes and to world leaders. He is recognized internationally and has experienced great success as a revivalist, an inspirational speaker, an author, and a church historian.

Roberts Liardon was born in 1966 in Tulsa, Oklahoma, as the first male child born to a student of the newly launched Oral Roberts University. His career in the ministry began at the young age of 12½ when he gave his initial public address. At 17, Liardon published his first book, *I Saw Heaven*, in which he related his experience of going to Heaven as a young boy. The book catapulted Roberts into the public eye and sold more than 1.5 million copies. Over the next few years, he became one of the leading public speakers in the Christian community all over the world.

When Roberts was 12½ years old, Jesus appeared to him in a vision and told him to study the great preachers — to learn both of their successes and failures. From that day on, Roberts began to devote himself to this study. This lifelong pursuit has established him as a leading Protestant Church historian, a role he carries with honor to this day.

The day came when God spoke further to Roberts about writing and producing both a DVD series and a book series entitled "God's Generals." The original mission was to chronicle the lives of some of the leading Pentecostal and Charismatic leaders so the Body could learn from both their successes and failures. The DVD series was an immediate success and became one of the bestselling Christian DVD series in the history of Christian media. The "God's Generals" book series is an ongoing assignment that also found a worldwide reading audience that has continued to grow over the years.

In 1990, Roberts Liardon moved to Southern California and founded his worldwide headquarters in Orange County. There he and his team founded Embassy Christian Center and Spirit Life Bible College, both of which became among the largest and most influential in the region.

In 2007, Roberts moved his ministry headquarters to Sarasota, Florida, where it is currently located. In 2009, he accepted the position as principal of the International Bible Institute of London, the training arm of the Kensington London City Church, a position he held for five years as an assignment from God to help further His plans and purposes for the United Kingdom and Europe.

Roberts Liardon continues to speak to this generation in pulpits across the United States and around the world. He also produces his own online courses, where he teaches on God's Generals and other key Bible truths necessary to strengthen the Body of Christ for this critical hour we live in.

Throughout the years, Roberts has continued to be a significant contributor toward building God's Kingdom, with the belief that relationships are the key element that bonds the staff at Roberts Liardon Ministries to people around the world. Each year millions are touched through this worldwide ministry, a genuine resource of victory for the entire Body of Christ.

CONTACT
ROBERTS LIARDON MINISTRIES

For further information
about Roberts Liardon Ministries,
please visit the ministry website at
www.robertsliardon.org

or contact us at:

U.S. Office:
Roberts Liardon Ministries
P.O. Box 4215
Sarasota, FL 34230
941-748-3883
Email: info@robertsliardon.org

Canada Office:
Roberts Liardon Ministries Canada
2A-13139 80 Ave.
Surrey BC V3W 3B1
604-594-7327
Email: info@robertsliardon.org

UK/Europe Office:
Roberts Liardon Ministries UK/Europe
22 Notting Hill Gate, Suite 125
London WII 3JE, England
Email: info@robertsliardon.org

Other ways to connect:

Facebook: Roberts Liardon Official
Twitter: @RobertsLiardon
Instagram: @robertsliardon_official
YouTube: Roberts Liardon

www.ingramcontent.com/pod-product-compliance
Lightning Source LLC
Chambersburg PA
CBHW072212070526
44585CB00015B/1305